When People Die

© Aladdin Books Ltd 2009

Designed and produced by
Aladdin Books Ltd

First published in 2009
in the United States
by Stargazer Books,
distributed by Black Rabbit Books
PO Box 3263
Mankato, MN 56002

Illustrator: Christopher O'Neill

The author, Sarah Levete, has written and edited many books for young people on social issues and other topics.

Printed in the United States

Library of Congress Cataloging-in-Publication Data

Levete, Sarah.
  When people die / Sarah Levete.
      p. cm. -- (Thoughts and feelings)
  Includes index.
  ISBN 978-1-59604-171-4
  1. Death--Psychological aspects--Juvenile literature. I. Title.
  BF789.D4L48 2009
  155.9'37--dc22
                              2008016389

When People Die

Sarah Levete

Stargazer Books

Mankato • Minnesota

Contents

Introduction

These children are all friends. They have all known someone who has died. Each of them had different feelings and reactions. There is lots of fear and mystery about death, though it is a natural part of life. Join these friends and other children as they discuss how they felt and how they coped when someone died.

When someone dies you have lots of confusing feelings.

Getting over the death of someone you love takes time.

People die for lots of different reasons.

If a friend is upset by a death, you can try to help comfort him or her.

Death And Dying

Aaron is showing his friend Phoebe a photo of his cat, Bogey, who died over the weekend. Aaron feels very sad and really misses Bogey. But he knows that every living thing must die some time. Bogey's body was not well enough to carry on living. Death is when the body stops working. People and animals are born, they live their lives, and then they die.

People are born. People grow up. People grow old.

You look really upset, Aaron. What's the matter?

My cat Bogey died over the weekend. That's a photo of her we took ages ago.

▶ Death Is Natural

If you look around your house or yard, you will see lots of living things. Each has been born and will die one day. Even a tree, which has lived for hundreds of years, may be blown down in a very strong wind and die.

◀ No Longer Working

When a person dies, his or her body stops working, like a toy that can't be mended. A toy no longer works because it is worn out. In the same way, a person may die because his or her body is too old to work anymore.

▶ What Is Dying?

A dying person is someone who is going to die soon. Most people expect to die when they get old, but some people die earlier because of a bad illness. It may take them months or years to die from an illness. A dying person needs care and support. But if you find it hard to see them, that's OK. A phone call can cheer them up too.

Aaron, tell us about your cat, Bogey.
"I feel really sad about Bogey dying. I miss her so much, but she was very old and her body was tired out. I know we couldn't have done anything more to help her. Mom says that dying is the most natural thing in the world. Everything that lives has to die--it's just how nature works."

Why Do People Die?

Erin recently joined Shelly's class at school. Erin is telling Shelly that her best friend, Eva, died from an illness. The doctors couldn't make her better. Shelly's uncle was killed in an accident two years ago. There are many reasons why people die. They may be ill or very old, or death may be caused by an accident.

Accidents cause injury and even death.

Do you have a best friend, Erin?

No. My best friend, Eva, died two months ago.

Story: A Short Life

1 When Bill's sister, Ally, was born, she wasn't very well.

2 The doctors tried giving her different medicines to make her better.

Come on, Ally, let's go outside.

Ally needs her medicine first.

She needs the medicine to make her well.

3 Ally died when she was three. Her body wasn't well enough to stay alive.

Why did Ally die?
Ally was ill for a long time. She didn't die suddenly. Her body slowly stopped working. The doctors tried to make Ally better but the different medicines didn't work. Sometimes people die very quickly. But it can take quite a long time, as it did for Ally.

▶ Illness

Sometimes you feel ill. In time your body heals itself, or you take medicine to make yourself feel better. But even medicine can't make some people well again— they may be too ill to get better.

I can't run like I used to.

◀ Old Age

Even after a long, healthy, and happy life, the body will get tired. In the end it will just stop working. But whatever the cause of death, people who were close to the person who has died will often feel very sad.

Today, two people died in a car crash.

▶ Accidents

Death can come without warning to healthy people. People may die in an accident, such as a car crash. Or they may die in a disaster, such as a flood. An accident can happen to a person who is young or old.

▶ Gone To Sleep?

Some grown-ups think it is better if young people don't understand about death. They may say that someone who has died has "gone to sleep" or "gone away." But death is not like sleep or going away, because the dead person will not wake up or come back. It is often better to be told the truth.

> But if he's gone away he'll come back.

◀ Don't Feel Guilty

You may feel worried or guilty if you said something rude or were mean to someone before he or she died. But you are not to blame. A person only dies because his or her body stops working.

> Did Grandad die because I didn't want him to stay at our house?

▶ Too Young...

Death is not just something that happens to people when they get old. Death can happen to anyone. However, it can be especially hard to cope with when the person who dies was still young.

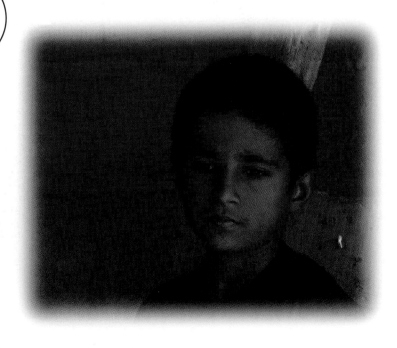

Shelly, how did your uncle die?
"My uncle died in a car accident. He was only forty. It seems so unfair. I used to think it was just old people who died, but it's not. Mom told me he had gone away, so I kept waiting for him to come back. But I knew something was wrong. In the end Mom told me the truth. I still felt sad, but at least I understood."

What Happens After Death?

At school, Lauren and Deepa are doing a project on different ideas about death. Nobody knows for sure what happens after death, but lots of people have strong beliefs. Whatever your beliefs, there are funerals and other ways that let you say a special goodbye to a person who has died. There are different kinds of burial as well.

Some people's bodies are buried…

What do you think happens when you die?

I think you have a spirit which lives on after your body dies.

…others are burned, or cremated.

14

▶ Saying Goodbye

Funerals and other customs can help you say goodbye to someone who has died. However, if you are worried about going to a funeral, ask an adult you trust to explain what is going to happen. If you decide not to go, you could write a letter to the person who has died to be buried with them.

I believe that souls go to heaven.

I believe that a person is reborn in heaven.

◀ Different Ideas

People have different beliefs about death. Some believe that everyone has a soul or spirit, which lives on when the body dies. Others believe that a person who has died is reborn as another person or animal. Some people think that a person who has died continues to live on in our memories.

▶ Burial Or Cremation

In most countries, people are taken to a special place after they die. The body may be buried in the ground or cremated—burned in a very hot fire. The ashes may be put in a place the person loved. Whatever happens to the body after death, it doesn't hurt— the body cannot feel anything.

Deepa, how did you feel about going to your grandad's funeral?
"Mom and Dad weren't sure if I should go to the funeral at first. I knew the funeral would be very sad, but I wanted to go and say goodbye to grandad properly. I talked it over with my mom and dad, and in the end they let me go. I'm glad I got a chance to say goodbye."

When Someone Dies

Charlotte and Lewis have been talking about how people feel when someone dies. Everyone reacts differently. A person's reaction depends on many things, such as how close they were to the dead person. Some people cry a lot. Others think it's better not to cry. Lewis' brother Joe died recently in a motorcycle accident. Lewis' mom found it hard to accept what had happened.

Crying helps you express how you feel.

Your brother's death was so sudden.

My mom still finds it hard to believe.

Your grandad had a long and happy life.

▶ In Shock

If someone dies very suddenly, relatives and friends may go into shock. They may feel numb, and find it difficult to believe what has happened. They may find it hard to eat or sleep. Other people don't feel much straight away. Their feelings may come out later.

▼ Sudden Or Expected

Some deaths are unexpected. Relatives and friends may feel upset they didn't say goodbye. Some deaths are more expected, because the person who has died was old or ill. A death which is expected may be easier to cope with than a sudden death.

I'm sorry, but I can't eat anything.

Lewis, how did your family react to Joe's death?
"Everyone reacted differently. Dad was very practical and organized everything for the funeral. Mom was in shock. I felt really upset, but didn't want to make things worse, so I tried not to show my feelings. At the funeral we all cried a lot and I felt a bit better afterward."

How Do You Feel?

Will is thinking about his grandma. It has been a few months since the funeral, but he still feels upset about his grandma's death. When someone dies, you may feel sad and miserable. You may feel angry. You may feel all of these, or just confused. These feelings are all part of a natural process called grieving. This is part of getting over someone's death.

You may find it hard to sleep at first.

I still feel sad about Grandma. I think I'll always miss her.

▶ ## Feeling Angry

At first you may feel angry with
the person who has died for
leaving you. You may feel he or
she has let you down. Or you
may feel angry with the person
who has died for making other
people sad. It's not unusual to
feel like this when someone dies.

◀ ## At School

If you are sad because someone has
died, you may find it hard to
concentrate at school. Feeling upset
can make you behave badly and get
into trouble. But taking out your
unhappy feelings on others won't
help. Talk to a teacher you trust and
explain what has happened.

▶ ## Talking Helps

Whether you feel sad,
upset, or angry, talking
about it will help. Don't
bottle up your feelings
inside. Try to tell a grown-
up or a good friend how
you feel. It won't make the
sad or difficult feelings go
away, but it can help you to
feel better.

▶ Feeling Confused

It can be difficult to see people upset at the death of a person they argued with. But people do argue, even when they love each other. Even if you didn't get on well with someone who died, your actions had nothing to do with the death.

It's not fair. Why was it my mom that died?

◀ It's Not Fair

It can seem unfair when someone close to you dies, especially if he or she was not old. You may feel angry that it was not someone else who died instead. But wishing it had happened to someone else will not help. Explain how you feel to someone you trust.

Will, how did you feel when your grandma died?

"At first I didn't really feel much when Grandma died. I cried more when our old dog died than when she died. But that didn't mean I didn't love her. Now, when we go to the park where Grandma used to take us, I really miss her."

Story: Feeling Scared

1 Sean's mom died a month ago. Sean didn't want his dad to go to work.

2 Sean felt too scared to sleep at night. He went downstairs to see his dad.

3 Sean's dad explained that he wasn't going to die and leave Sean too.

Why was Sean scared?

Sean's mom had died when she was young. Sean was frightened that his dad might die as well. It is quite natural to feel scared if a parent or carer dies. If you are worried about who will look after you, talk about your worries to a grown-up who is close to you.

Hailey persuaded Connor to join in a game. Connor told Hailey that after his dad's death he didn't want to play with anyone. But Connor's mom told him that he could still remember his dad even if he was having fun. If someone dies, you will have lots of different feelings. You will start feeling better, although it may take a long time.

One minute you may feel sad.

The next minute you may feel OK.

I'm glad you decided to play.

So am I. I didn't want to at first.

► Show Your Feelings

If someone close to you has died, you may have lots of difficult feelings, including anger, sadness, and loneliness. Don't hide your feelings. It may help to make a model out of clay, or paint a picture to show how you feel.

Why did he have to die? It's so unfair.

◄ Feeling Better

Sometimes you have to accept a situation, even though it may not be what you want. If you talk to your parent about your feelings, he or she will be able to understand how you feel about the situation.

► Special Occasions

Birthdays and other special occasions can make you feel very sad. If you miss the person who has died, you could draw them a picture or write them a letter. You may also find that it helps to talk in your head to the person who has died.

Story: Mixed Feelings

1 Isha's sister died in an accident. Isha felt sad and guilty at the same time.

2 One day Isha heard her mom and dad saying how good Bella always was.

> Bella was such a good girl. I still miss her so much.

> But Bella was naughty sometimes, too. Don't they love me?

3 Later Isha told her best friend, Ali, about what she had heard.

What can Isha do?

Isha should talk to her parents about how she feels. When someone dies, people often remember just the good things. Of course Isha's parents miss Bella, but that doesn't mean that they don't love Isha. If you feel miserable and left out because someone has died, try talking about your feelings with a grown-up who you trust.

▶ Moving On

If someone who was close to you has died, you may feel that you shouldn't enjoy yourself. You may feel guilty about having fun. But you can still have strong feelings for the person who has died, and live your life fully. It's OK to feel happy and make new friends.

◀ Show You Care

If you know someone whose friend or relative has died, try to imagine how he or she must be feeling. Make a special effort to be understanding and caring toward that person. You can help by making sure they don't feel left out.

Hailey, how should you behave to someone who is grieving?
"There's no right or wrong way to behave. My best friend is Connor. His dad died a few weeks ago. At first I didn't know what to say to him. I felt uncomfortable. Mom said to be myself but be kind. If you know someone who has lost a friend or relative, you can help by showing you care."

Don't Forget...

1

Did you ever feel confused when your grandad died, Deepa?

"I felt lots of different things when Grandad died. It was really confusing, but it helped me to talk to my parents about it. Sometimes now when I feel sad it can help me feel better if I draw a picture."

2

Do you still think about your cat, Aaron?

"If a person or animal you love dies, you will feel very sad. After a time, you stop feeling quite so sad. But that doesn't mean that you forget the person or animal. I've got a new cat, Bluey, now. I really like her, but I still miss Bogey. I remember the good times we had."

3

Does it take long to get over the death of someone you were close to, Lewis?
"Getting over the death of a friend or relative may take a long time. To begin with, you may not want to play with friends. But in the end, you will feel better and have good memories about happy times you shared with the person who has died."

4

Hailey, how can you help if you know someone whose friend or relative has died?
"If you know someone who is grieving, be especially kind to him or her. It can make a big difference if you show you care, even if your friend isn't ready to play or to have fun yet. When you are unhappy, friends can really help to make you feel better."

Find Out More About Dealing With Death

Helpful Addresses and Phone Numbers

Talking about problems and worries can really help. If you can't talk to someone close to you, then try phoning one of these organzations:

Association for Death Education and Counseling
342 North Main Street
West Hartford,
CT 06117-2507
Tel: (860) 586-7503

Compassionate Friends
PO Box 3696
Oak Brook,
IL 60522-3696
Tel: (630) 990-0010

The Compassionate Friends of Canada
PO Box 141, RPO Corydon
Winnepeg, MB R3M 3S7
Tel: (866) 823-0141
Email: tcfcanada@aol.com

The Dougy Center
3909 SE 52nd Avenue
PO Box 86852
Portland, OR 97268
Tel: (503) 775-5683

The National Board for Certified Counselors
3D Terrace Way
Greensboro, NC 27403
Tel: (910) 547-0607

On the Web

These websites are also helpful. You can get in touch with some of them using email:

www.adec.org

www.compassionatefriends.org

www.tcfcanada.net

www.dougy.org

www.grief-recovery.com

wwwgriefworksbc.com.

www.kidzworld.com/site/p4027.htm

www.rainbows.org

Further Reading

If you want to read more about dealing with death and grief, try:

Let's Talk About: Death and Dying by Bruce Sanders (Stargazer Books)

Choices and Decisions: When People Die by Pete Sanders and Steve Myers (Stargazer Books)

How Can I Deal With: When People Die by Sally Hewitt (Franklin Watts)

Wipe Out by Mimi Thebo (Collins)

Michael Rosen's Sad Book by Michael Rosen (Walker Books)

What On Earth Do You Do When Somebody Dies? by Trevor Romain and Elizabeth Verdick (Free Spirit Publishing)

Index

Photocredits